TWO LEAVES IN AUTUMN

VATSAL SHARMA

First published in 2018 by

Becomeshakespeare.com

Wordit Content Design & Editing Services Pvt Ltd
Unit - 26, Building A -1, Nr Wadala RTO,
Wadala (East), Mumbai 400037, India
T: +91 8080226699

Wordit Art Fund helps deserving authors publish
their work by providing monetary support.
To apply for funding, please visit us at
www.BecomeShakespeare.com

ISBN - 978-93-88573-74-0

About The Author

Vatsal Sharma is a young, upcoming poet and author who writes masterfully in English and Urdu. He has been mesmerising and impressing his readers for a few years now with his wordplay and skill around the languages. His maiden collection of poems in English is a testament to love which throws all the conventions out the window as an 18 year old sets words in a way that they play a beautiful and sometimes haunting harp with your heartstrings.

Acknowledgement

More people than I can name should be rewarded with utmost respect for this work that has shaped me as an artist. Beginning with family: my brother, Mansvi who helped me at every point in my life, and taught me how to use the voice that I inherited, not just this book, the thought of me coming up with something of my own would have been impossible without him; my mother, Mamta Sharma and father, Narendra Sharma, who at every step in their lives did whatever was right for my future, it is impossible to thank them in words; my sister Kalyani who reviewed each and every poem with honesty and helped me in every way she could, whether related to writing or any personal matter; my dear friend Yagya who gave me a purpose when I needed it the most. I am also very grateful to my friends Bhavya Sharma and Arka Routh who captured and edited the cover of this book and made it more attractive. And so many more people that I cannot name because of many reasons, but I am grateful to each and every person who buys this book and thus tries to promote poetry and art in whole.

Dedication

Contents

Pehle humaare zehn mein husn ki ek misaal thi
Ab toh humaare zehn mein koi misaal bhi nahi

Jaun Elia

The life of lights that I never knew,
And the life of lights that never knew me.

0

Offering

Oh sweet name how I see you,
At every venue, old or new,
You emerge from light and coo,
In existence of dark and blue.

But, I see your grace everywhere,
How the words walk with me,
And find shadows in my despair,
That begins and ends with thee[1].

May I hear never your voice,
And I never get you in whole,
For sweet, oh sweet it is not a choice,
It is to what literature I owe:
So here by I offer you immortality,
With my gentle words for your tender soul.

[1.] you

1

Your Words Haunt Me

Your words haunt me.
The words that you forced out in the moment,
ones that you never said,
words that gave birth to the nights of talk
that were to be, but never were,
and the promises that in their hearts had
words that made me feel safe.

And they still haunt me, after days and nights
of you proving your words wrong,
they haunt me for my own words for you,
dear poem,
always in their heart had faith and truth,
but my words you never heard,
my words that you never read,
haunt me because they echo in me
like a dying call for help;
they haunt me like a childhood song
that I cannot remember.
My words have turned against me,
like a coin that stood still for a second,
and I now stand still giving birth
to more mornings that will not end.

But, your words haunt me,
they always will.
The new definitions you invented,
how home did not remain home:
how home is in the air.
Your words haunt me, now and then,
And sadly, they are all I have,
no memories, no pictures, no curtains
that make the sun flicker[1],
just words that hold me, in afternoons
on my bed, on the road, in my sleep,
words that gently conquer my dreams.

But, word is not world,
though it is for me.
And I wallow in the murmurs
of promises that couldn't be,
of poems that never were.

So, here I give back to you,
promises of the evenings.

[1.] unsteady shining of a light

2

O My Muse

O my muse[1]
For my words are powerful
and your eyes are the reason.
I write with a mere pen
and you guide my hand.
You guide my hand into turning ink
to an immortal meaningful life.
See me, for I am a mere machine
and you are the essential dew-like fuel.
In the starry night, when my eyes are lonesome
you stare into my heart and present me
with the true eternal idea of life.
Oh, I am a fool to think
that a man can tame your heavenly body.

[1] a person who inspires art

3

O Light Of My Life

O light of my life,
let me smell the dawn
through your silent flailing[1] hair.
You stand alone, picking flowers
and passing your perfume of life.

Watching you, work like a butterfly,
the sunny day turns into
a melancholy night of love.
My love rises through the abyss[2]
of hatred, and falls into you.
You make my every day,
into a night of poem and love.

When I was a child, I sat by a lake,
amidst the mist and singing the song of silence,
felt the greater things in life, and left the common blisses;
you, now completed the picture with your simple smile.

I see you in the stars, the sun, the moon,
you are like a lovely excuse that lives on.
Love creates a life in itself;
I see you, and a world is born,

[1] wave wildly, [2] bottomless chasm

too beautiful to be real, and oh, the blisses;
I cry still, to live in reality.

Oh, the world falls like dew from your eyes,
on the tips of your name.
May your beauty live long enough to die,
and may my ink last long enough to love you.

4

If I Were An Artist

If I were an artist,
I would paint you: in *rouge*[1].
Like your scarlet[2] hair,
and brown eyes:
I would create something infinite.

I would pour the colour on you,
and the painting would complete itself.
O the mother of painters and poets!
A thousand artists were born,
the day you rose through the dawn.

You paint the world, and here I sit: painting you.
How do I complete your divine portrait?

My lamp in the night: I love you.

If I were an artist,
I would paint you: in *bleu*[3].
Like the night of full moon,
and like the wine in my cup.

[1.] red, [2.] red, [3.] blue

The colour of night and melancholy:
with a touch of love:
O how do I describe?

In my tub of beauty,
you will pose:
like a diamond in the
bleu ocean.

O the mother of painters and poets!

If I were an artist,
I would paint you: in monochrome[1].
Like the last night with the beloved,
and like standing in the desolated rain.

In the colour, that is simple as your eyes:
you shall be the portrait of a lovely night.
The roses are black, like everything else:
there you shine like the sun:
O illuminations like that of a firefly:
do not die so soon.

Like the rivers in a gloomy day,
and the abandoned temples:
you are the uncertain beauty I love.

O what should I choose?
You look like the dusk[2] in *rouge*,
dawn in *bleu,*

[1] black and white, [2] after sunset and just before night.

and the night in monochrome.
O what should I choose
I am a fool to paint you in one colour,
whilst[1] the rainbow rises from you.

1. while

5

Let Me Sing

Let me sing
the song that is you.
Think not that I am waving you
like a prize;
I am just singing like the birds
sing the coming of spring,
like the land celebrates the coming
of autumn to mate with the leaves.

Let me write a song for your eyes:
an endless song that is sung by rivers,
mountains, seas and the flute.

Let me celebrate your existence;
like the people celebrate god.

I walk in the festivals;
and my everyday is a festival.

I light a lamp in front of your eyes,
it lasts longer to sing the
luminous grace that you are.

I hear the song of everything:
fire, water, trees, storms
and they sing for you.
O were they your lovers?

Clouds blush and stars wink
in the distance
when at night you sing the song
that is love.

Let me sing a song for which:
the roses open, the clouds rain,
the sun rises and I-
I contain your love.

6

In The Cold Winter Night

In the cold winter night,
while sleeping on the right,
I feel my dreams hollow,
I wake up, and you are gone.

I go out as I shiver
in the cursed thoughts of love;
and your dark horse stands
in the cruel storm.
'O my friend,
maybe you know where she is.'

I ride on your horse,
it walks past the woods,
and leaves me by an endless
frozen lake;
O this is where I must
live, now.

I see your horse weeping,
and I hear from his breath:
'O brother, cry not,
for it's both of our lives
that has left.'

7

Dear Bird

Oh dear bird where have you fled?
Through my windowpane I saw you,
chirping and singing of life;
silently gathering the morning,
from the lost fragments of night,
and waking the fields and sun
by taking them on a modest flight.
And beyond here rests nothing,
there is a vast forest,
where all is found and nothing is;
many ponds, many lakes, many rivers,
and a sky so blue that the sun,
is like a lighthouse in a sea,
and the clouds, the icebergs,
that rain of secluded life;
oh, you must have fled there,
leaving your feather gatherer behind,
and I am left with this
garland of feathers and leaves,
that once touched you.
Another day another bird will come,
and build a nest bit by bit,
each night I will come out,
and steal that nest from the bough:

I will do it every time till,
you come back and I will offer you,
a field of nests, so you will live,
in a different house each time,
and suffice your wandering mind.

8

My Ink Is Gone

My ink is gone
and the pen is dry.
Waiting for me to
write another lie.
And my soul can't
write this cry.
The time has come
for my words to die.

My hand stutters
when I pick the pen.
I sit and drink
like all the men.
Wine speaks the truth
every now and then.
'Give me back my muse'
and God says, 'Amen.'

I am dead and hollow,
yes I confess.
Don't touch my feet
for I can't bless.
My words lost the meaning
and that killed me, yes.
The rain is out
but, I can't express.

9

I Still See

I still see those gardens you create,
with just one simple smile.
And thus, in the sleepless nights,
I continue to write,
so you will wake up reading and smiling,
and then I will go to sleep smiling,
knowing you and I exist at one moment,
and in my dreams I will walk,
to you in the garden,
with everything turning monochrome[1] and still,
with words becoming rhymes and music natural:
together, we will win life and change time,
travel together to the days we have heard of,
when life was free and fields were open,
I shall have you then, you shall have me.

[1] black and white

10

Now I Know

Now I know why drops of water
clasp[1] around your waist.
And even the dry cloth finds salvation,
being rubbed against your skin.
Oh, it is like I have stepped in
a mountain of fog since I looked at you,
and a sea of laments[2] and mourning lanterns.
My hand trembles when I cast my fingers
around the lining of your skin,
and each moment my hand buries itself deeper,
in the abyss of your body, that I wish to fall in.

I now am disquiet[3], seeing you without silk,
around your body, of milk.
But, so have I found the bliss finally,
for I know the eternal secret, that,
why drops of water clasp around your waist

[1.] grasp tightly, [2.] a passionate expression of grief, [3.] a feeling of unease

11

I Like You To Flicker

I like you to flicker:
like a candle battling the wind,
and like a light in the distant dark land.

With your eye staring in the dark,
and hands feeling helpless:
I lay the smoky ice on your skin,
the mist rises when you and ice mate,
you tremble as you melt the ice,
and the waters flow from you.
It is like your soul has shaken:
I like you to flicker.

When you have befriended ice,
and you breathe for the next moment:
in the dark, I light a candle:
it illuminates the room, like you
illuminate the world.

Near your trembling body, I bring it,
the candle bows to you and,
its holy fuel falls on you:
you ache like a sad song.

You, innocent rose, you have
plucked yourself from the
orchard, and given yourself to me:
even though you know what I am.
Now, here I am, trying to cherish
you through my wicked ways of love.

Like a fire in the dark forest,
and like a young babe unaware of herself.
I like you to flicker.

12

I'm Here, Dear Poem

I'm here, dear poem.
You can now leave the temporary arrangement,
and come with me
so we'll drive into a sunset,
without a car,
without a sunset.

13

Night Affair

A night-affair, shall last for a night,
without a question, you shall depart[1],
from their eyes;
say goodbye, once, look not back,
and kiss the heavens for present of the night.

If you shall look back, you will be trapped,
in the affair they call the life;
the affair of life, is not easy, not bright,
it is hard, and greater than your might.
There is no goodbye, just a hello each time,
and a smile that talks like the river-song.

For I shall not tell you what you shall do,
just in the night affair, while making love,
whisper in each other's ear,
for love is playing music, beautiful, divine,
and you shall respect it each minute of your life.

[1] leave

14

Was I Just A Drop Of Water

Was I just a drop of water
in your cloud of lovers?
For me, you were my water,
and I was falling in your soul,
deeper and deeper, to find,
an end to your beauty.
Still I am falling into the depth
where colours have no meaning;
it's you: it is you: just you.
I wish I had me, with you.

To find the tavern[1] where,
you are the barmaid[2] of love,
I am falling with bliss[3];
years and years hence,
I shall fall still,
for my heaven rests in
the tavern of your eyes,
where the wine of satisfaction
flows, and flows, and flows.

[1] a place where alcohol is sold. [2] a woman serving in a bar. [3] perfect happiness.

15

Last Wish

Happiness is just two pages,
it is these memories that live for ages.
Your memory, a shadow, dark,
hollow, immsense, that visits me,
at times it wishes.

To run my hands through your hair,
I still dwell on the pages;
like water, you are simple
and necessary for me;
and like the wine,
you are an addiction.

The birds fly over my soul,
to the rotting hills of bliss.
I sit alone in the dark,
and now the sadness seems erotic.

In the evenings, still sometimes,
the wind passes through me,
with its moistness, I am reminded,
of your sweet lips, like a harp.

The song that you sang, in me,
had no meaning: like love.
You danced, with your wet garment
and majestic smile in my thoughts,
and owned the land of dreams,
to dance for eternity.

I shall butcher the hearts
of a million women,
without touching their body,
I shall hold them by their soul;
for they wish they could
remind me of you.

But, visions remind me of you;
melancholic voice, whispers,
and the wild.

So when I am in my deathbed,
telling the beads of your lovely name,
do not smile back: I want to breathe more.
Do not take me under your shadow
of inevitable agony,
for even the infidels honour the last wish.

16

Firework

She carried a plate of lamps in her hands,
I watched her work silently,
like she was serving wine to me;
on the day when night was awaited,
she lit the night: and the heavens kissed bright;
I watched her work, without awareness,
of the fire that burns through her shadows,
under her shadow I live, without desires,
and eternally free of sorrows.

The sky is spread through the night,
and the stars don't glitter bright,
with her hands and their might,
she holds the calmness within her light;
a firework she lights illuminates
the sky, and the sorrows hide.
She is the firework I light,
and I am the shadow beneath her light.

The lamps of her night shine through the day,
and nights are awaited deeply,
for in the dark only do we appreciate the light.

17

Two Leaves In Autumn

To the end that awaits us,
on the stop where we depart.
I walk and carry still your smile,
deep within a shy vein that hides,
for it's too seldom[1] now to feel the bliss
within you and within my muse's sighs.
I can't begin to cry, for I don't know how,
and your eyes must not do so,
or I shall have everything sacrificed.
All the dying voices whisper gently,
your name through the streets.
Like every bleeding arrow,
like every river that ends.

In the memories of our meeting,
and the sighs of departure,
rest both of our mistakes.
Like a storm you burnt my fire,
and left me with the ashes,
that still blow within your hauling[2] wind,
and I walk behind them,

[1.] rare, [2.] pull with force

hoping they are embers, but I cannot catch them,
neither do I want to.
Like every night after the dawn,
like every struggle of an infant.

The two leaves that we were,
from very different trees,
I: from a tree of thorns, while,
you: from the cherry tree,
and yet we met beyond the boundaries of despair;
to fall on each other in autumn,
and live the tomorrow too,
I tangled within your scent,
and breathed all of your essence.
But, now the wind is hauling,
like there is no tomorrow,
and you are flying towards the sea,
of endless possibilities, I am following you:
like I promised.
Within the fate and destiny untold,
the two leaves in autumn have finally departed.
Like every bird lost,
like every wine drop spilled.

18

Howling Wind

Sorrows laughing into me,
they're biting each and every strand,
of my past, a rusty hammer, with a nail,
to get through my cover of saneness;
yes, you, oh mother of ignorance,
where were you when I was burned,
beneath your distance and rest,
but, you leaned into the fire,
and burnt my soul as I dreamt,
of your incense of the morning;
it's now too late for you,
to rise within the ashes,
of my fate.
Even though, one day you rose,
through the distance,
and ceased my wait to flow,
and I held you again in my arms,
as I closed my eyes of dreams,
I opened with the very eyes of truth,
I have lived in the dreams,
and now I dwell[1] through the nightmare's mud.
But, in the distance, someone is laughing,

[1] live

for I've waited too long,
I see my sorrows and desires walking,
through the howling wind.
Knives are now surpassing my thoughts,
each time I think of your pretty face.
The wine that I drink,
is the last one each time I pay,
but, the cup is hollow,
and it echoes your name as I pour the wine,
to not remember you is all I have tried,
but, to not remember you: I can't suffice
the soul that feeds on the fire you lit,
with your hands like water,
and threw me in the mould of your filth,
to change my shape, and arranged me as you will;
oh, lovely lady, oh sad eyed bird,
walk no lands, for now I am done,
to wait for your firmness and kindness
like the devil, I shall go to heaven,
and light all the taverns,
that I built in your memory.
Now the poems are being sung,
by some kids who wish to cling to the fruit,
that defines that they are young;
yet, you will walk, I know you will,
for the game I am is endless yet complete,
and you play with all your tricks,
that have worked a million times,
and a million more, yes they will.

I've waited too long,
in the red summer evening,
for you to come on your horse,
and to rise with your silhouette[1],
through the howling wind.

[1]. the dark shape and outline of someone or something visible in restricted light against a brighter background

19

Sinking Of The Sea

In the night there is a sea,
where bright things have no company,
I dwell[1] and breathe in the night,
to catch a glimpse of your emerald[2] sight.
In the night as I continue to brood[3],
I hear the echo of my name in my solitude[4],
you chanting my name when the stars have set,
I run to the waterfall where we met:
like a painting, as you bathe:
again in the moonlight: I have been scathed[5].

Oh you lay the bed of memories with fire,
I find an end to this endless pyre[6],
between the departure and meeting it tingles,
as I extinguish the scent of hope I see the embers[7] twinkle.
With all the ugliness in me: I groan,
only to trap myself again, in your lovely moan.
But, in the night beneath your ashes I dwell,
and in the day I can't find a hand in this dell[8],

[1.] live, [2.] a bright green colour, [3.] think deeply, [4.] the state of being alone, [5.] harmed, [6.] a large pile of woods on which a dead body is burnt, [7.] piece of burning coal in a dying fire,[8.] a small valley among trees

you may evade[1] me when you see my conscience yell,
but, it is I and I who knows both heaven and hell.

I still remember each blink of your eyes,
your creation of fire and ice,
your nights of endless mourning,
and your morn[2] of sun's blessing:
to be fiery[3] like the northern star, and calm like the sinking
sun,
and show your light to the ones whom god has shun[4].
In the world that is a stage,
you are a story that shall never age.

I was searching on and on in the field of flower,
and as I bathed under god's lovely shower,
there I saw walking a name I once wrote in the sand,
oh a flower walked by flowers to hold my hand,
under the song of rain as I stood:
I found the oblivion of my childhood.
Now I brood while tangling under night's scent:
how did I lose infinity in a moment?

I only cherish the cup of wine,
to rise through this endless pine[5].
I live in the delirium[6] of a dream,
for only I shall see you in the moonbeam.
Beneath the weight of your kisses I think,
of the time when my life was in pink,
and among the stars I was the only one,
to have kissed the farthest sun.

1. ignore, 2. morning, 3. burning strongly, 4. ignore, 5. mental and physical decline, 6. illusion

When life fed on mountains of grief huge,
it was then under your silk I found refuge.
I frown upon our meeting,
for it is I alone who is now bleeding.
I throw the weeping cup on the floor,
only to create another deeper door:
I enter into an endless room adorned[1] by azure[2] light,
and I fall into your lap like a dead kite;
I pray you and cherish you then,
and make love to you like my solitary yen[3].
Through you I look beyond the rising sun without a memory,
towards the sinking of the sea,
where life is greater than the dream,
you are the night, you are the gleam,
where your blooming thoughts are also free:
I will take you there, if you will take me.

[1] decorated, [2] colour of cloudless sky, [3] yearning

20

Tell Me, O Muse

Tell me, O muse of your glittering eyes.
Bright star, with your dance of alchemy,
turn wood into gold, stone into sapphire,
and melancholy into blissful.
You are mine, with all the birds and rivers singing.
I howl your name at sunsets and morns[1],
till you put me to sleep,
and in my dreams:
I howl your name at sunsets and morns.

I pick the flowers that steal your breath,
and on they go in the rivers where women bathe,
to gain your incense.
It is of your eyes that speak a language
full of love and sadness,
and its songs makes the fire still.

I worship your silence each night,
under the stars you lay and,
kiss their lonesome illuminations till they die;
children, men, women pray for the dying star,
but, living till eternity it gained peace at last.

[1] mornings

O where did I find you first?
In mist? In rain, or in the day?
Maybe, in the smoke of past,
or an unremembered dream.
But, you had been with me,
as I stepped through shadows,
and walked into days;
you held my hand through time.

21

You

You,
you who could make the generations tremble,
for whom the generations should tremble,
you who is unseen yet, you who is unknown,
you who has found me, yet not found me yet,
you who are dying, you who never lived,
think not, the time will not remember you,
as I was once told in one of my visions,
god talked to you and said,
'You want the generations to love you,
so here it is:'
and I opened my eyes.

22

Myriad Miles

Myriad[1] miles I have walked, searching for an answer,
on green roads and bright streets,
on misty mountains and giant fleets[2].
To find the answer that is in you,
I have found the shore of my emptiness.
I walk far from you, and reach closer,
I run faster, and the time becomes slower;
Oh, you've taken everything.
Leave not the poet disquiet:
for he may make you immortal.
My question is an answer to eternity,
so, one night come in my dreams,
and tell me, O muse:
"Teri aankhe kavita mein yaa teri aankho mein kavita?"

[1.] countless number, [2.] groups of ships sailing together

23

Universe

What all is left of me, belongs to you,
and a fraction of your universe is where I dream to reside,
under the million stars of your past,
I shall lay on the grass and
toast for the night of departure may never come.
A thousand souls and dreams and sighs and kisses,
within you find home.
And a million words and poems and books and paintings,
are created by each breath of yours.
Sighs and sighs, beyond the point I could rise,
and smile to the sun, that may never drown again.
Shadows of mine bring me down,
but, in the sea of time, you are my lighthouse.
I see today and tomorrow in you, and each moment,
dies while celebrating the next.
Each day is a festival, each lamp is immortal,
each crime is forgiven, each life is cherished;
no lover is forsaken, no infant is awaken,
no death is mourned, no poet is stoned.
Surrounded by the mist of your pale body,
the mountains stand tall,
and through the petals of your arms,
the dew falls into the souls of believers.

May all my bliss be blessed by your smile,
and all my crimes fall at your feet.

In you is the universe of the naked.

49

24

Happiest Flowers

How do I remind myself of you
when you never leave?
In each thought you live, and
in each regret and desire.
All I have are thoughts to brood[1],
and dreams to sow;
I have counted my days in kisses:
and re-lived each of them
under the memory of your shadow.
Every night I think:
each babe born should utter your name,
and each man dying should do the same.
And, when I see a lavish white villa,
I think of you,
but, oh, the happiest flowers are found
in the open fields.

[1] think deeply

25

Roses Are Red

Roses are red,
Violets are blue,
Evening knows that,
And water too.

Roses are red,
Violets are blue,
People are regular,
And you are you.

Roses are red,
Violets are blue,
You have not met me,
Though have I met you?

Roses are red,
Violets are blue,
At the top of a mountain,
Me and you.

Roses are red,
Violets are blue,
You love me,
I love you too.

26

O Who Are You

O who are you?
And why do I find myself smiling each time I think of you?
Though, you know not who I am:
I know who you are:
you are what I saw in the painful
smoke of past which each day became a cloud
and rained of agony over my tomorrow;
you were the desire to forget the smoke.

And why am I fascinated by you?
For I have found myself in your eyes
where every sad song is sung with a smile.
Why do I not know you?
And why do you not know me?
Is it for you to run till I catch you
on the shore of idea of love?
Or for you are the holy feather in a storm
that I must chase?

Forgive my inability to describe,
for you have taken words like
lovely, beautiful for your toenail.
What shall I even say for your deadly face?
Maybe, I will create a language,

where every word is a poem,
and is sung by the lips;
where meanings are meaningless.
And where every poem is lost
in your eyes from where it came.

27

La Douleur Exquise

In the night when I couldn't find you

I shivered to sleep, for the nightmare may end.

And each time it did,

for the dawn of bliss rose through you.

But, now how did I lose something I never had?

Under your spell, I remained writing,

or I created this spell of yours under which I now die.

I have more memories of you than

the weight of your rigid heart.

But, you do not have one.

How could you?

You are not even aware of my existence.

La douleur exquise[1]:

Oh, I've been a fool.

[1] the exquisite pain

28

What Separates Us

If I could step in your heart,
I would find myself standing,
in a vast field of flowers.
If you could step in my heart,
you would find yourself standing,
in your own shadow,
in which is the field of flowers.

Even though cities and life separate us,
each night they turn into a garden,
where we walk, hand in hand.
All I see is you and you and you,
you look like everyone else to me,
or everyone else looks like you?

How do I end a poem for you
when you don't hear any line?
But, somewhere you are struggling,
on the slippery slope of sighs,
and I am waiting and waiting
for you to be broken once again,
so that you will be healed
by reading my poem that ends with
your smile turning cities into a garden.

29

My Soul Echoes

My soul echoes like in a *haveli* when I think of you,
and each time I pray, your eyes beg me,
to call out their names as well, oh the fools!
How could I pray for an ocean lost in its own sky?
I breathe to count each night with you,
the nights were short, but oh each moment tells a thousand
lost stories.
And I never slept, and heard every story of yours,
and I don't remember them,
for the beauty of the unsung is freedom.
I need know about your past, the tale of every scar,
so we could wash them together from the moon of your skin.
In you I found every sunset, rain and dawn,
but as I go looking for autumn, I fail!
Oh, come and begin the spring by
kissing flowers and mercy at your feet.

What do I say of you, O stranded stranger?
Every lost boat on the shore of your beginning finds salvation.
And even the desert sand clasps around your pale feet;
so what am I, a rolling stone in your garden:
have I known every inch of you.
Each bird that sings for home thinks of you,
each firefly that dies lights itself
like a candle in your soul,

and each flower that blossoms thinks of you
instead of the butterflies.
So what am I, just a poem in your book:
your name is hidden in the silence between words.

My words have now grown older,
and you, my distant desire have become younger;
how shall I do justice to you?
You could compromise, or guide your poet,
on the path of immortals that begins in your eyes.

I feel a thousand things when I think of you,
a star falls and I pray, a child is born and I cherish.
You have balanced everything on your eyelashes.
It is like I have stepped in an abandoned home,
and every wall tells a new story.
Let me be the listener of your tales,
and the watcher of your stars.

Oh, I am not just saying this,
you stepped in my dreams long ago,
now spread your fragrance when the morning comes.
Oh, you feel like an ancient land,
my life turns monochrome,
when I think of you.
God, help me, I think too much, babe.

So, on your lovely lips take my name once again,
and I will head into its eternal echo like in a *haveli*.

30

In Cities

I was walking like the wandering dust,
and I touched a thousand trees,
and tasted myriad[1] fruits,
I smelled each flower: withered or blooming.
From waterfalls to bridges,
from gardens to concrete jungles,
and thus in the depressing buildings,
I found a flower standing in its own soil.
Oh, I believed, each poem shall begin,
in the woods, where flute sings of silence,
and under the waterfalls, I shall find,
the light of heaven, falling at my feet;
but, oh I was wrong, too wrong.

Here, are the streets I despise,
and the shops I loathe,
and the songs I ignore,
and a web through which I can travel the world;
and then a poem misplaced,
in the book of numbers;
oh, who wrote you?
Or are you like the rain,
that writes itself,

---

[1] countless

or the warm summer,
that dries ink to immortality,
or the freezing winter,
where every icicle[1] writes your poem,
or the happy spring,
where every flower hides in your book.

But, oh, with you I'll walk in these streets,
till I breathe the air that you breathe,
and till I see the sun that you see,
and till I kiss the roses off your lips.
And if you want to escape, then we can close our eyes,
to see how life changes when we are together,
each day will turn into a night,
and each night into a lovely poem.
Oh, I've lived in the woods for too long,
but, finally in you I have found,
a garden so simple that its vastness,
disappears into itself; and I walk till the end,
to find a flower blooming with my name.

Together, we create two leaves tangled in each other:
the very basic idea of nature.

[1.] a hanging piece of ice formed by the freezing of dripping water

31

Street Lights

You are so far, oh lovely bird,
it is like you are the sun of my eyes,
I can see you when I close them,
but, you are gone as I open them.

And you do create suns and moons,
each time you visit me in my dreams;
oh, there you are the queen,
and the princess, and the farmer;
you are everything, you are everywhere.
I am another sad light in your modern city,
cars drive past me, and I remain unseen,
but, oh, with you, my love, I feel happy,
the very idea of phosphenes[1]:
rose through the oblivion in your eyes.
I am a distant light each time you see me,
oh, I never come near you,
for how can I come near you?
I come from the moon, and the sun,
and the stars; I am the light.
But, to come near you, is another dream,
that I laugh at in the twilight.
My life is my dream, your eyes have taken me,

[1] an impression of light that occurs without light entering the eye

and forgive me, if I ever mistake your name with life,
for it is the deepest breath that screams,
of the solitude where we are one, and alone.
The distant voice is now approaching,
your car is now stopping,
under my light in the dark, desolated street,
but, no I don't feel different or excited.
And now I know why.
You are everything, you are everywhere.

32

Anklets

Look at those anklets of your feet smile and shine,
to hug around the pillar of forgiveness and love,
the beginning of salvation that rests in the dust,
under your pale feet where lives the seraphic dove
wallowing in the mud, sinking, sinking in the lust.

And I wish again, to see the moon shine through,
the diamonds of your anklets;
and I wish again, for the night to turn dark and blue.
All my bliss is momentary, and you are the moment,
with every memory of mine lost in your simple wine,
I still always find lamps burning in my land of lament[1],
as I look at those anklets of your feet smile and shine.

[1.] a passionate expression of grief

33

We Are Far

Oh, muse, we are far,
but, see I am walking the lands you once walked;
the same tea-stall, the same roads and sceneries,
different visions, ecstasies and sadness.
The time for worries and sadness is over:
I am buying all your problems.

And thus, if you think of me once,
just say it to the wind,
I will come running,
for only a fool would ignore,
a flower's invitation hidden,
in fragrance of a butterfly.

34

Lovely Lady

Lovely lady, where are you?
I've searched every flower,
and every lost poem,
yet, still in depth of every hour,
when my thoughts become yours,
I see your skin shine under sun's shower.
I've been so lost in the garden of your beauty,
O how do you not know of your young power?

What am I, just a poet,
lost under the blue sky,
in the infinite simple field,
untouched by modernity's sigh,
still looking for you,
while you hide in my every cry,
and I pull from roots the flowers,
till even their seeds die;
searching for the truth,
have I found a lie,
so beautiful that my field of dreams,
rests in its unsung black eye.

35

I Saw Your Feet Touch The Grass

I saw your feet touch the grass,
and I saw the garden smile vast,
the picture was small, of your pale feet,
but, in it I saw the whole world alas!
The lining of the heart, that surrounded your feet,
was glowing with red or blue fire at last;
and I always thought as the heart would open,
there I will see your feet shining on the grass!

Forgive me for not telling I write for you,
and for unwillingly sending you in immortal class.
And I will remain writing on the street,
of your old city hoping you will pass,
blame me not, oh perfect name,
for I have seen your feet touch the grass.

36

Tale

A garden of night with shades of roses sprinkled,
And a few dew drops of morning becoming stars,
A white city, never seen, that hides beneath it,
Waits to be touched by the sweet sun,
Spring that left, fragrance that lives here,
Ribbons that dance with the wind at each end,
Soft like a poet's quill, sweet like a gentle touch,
And dense like a forest that never ends,
Some blessed ones fall together,
Looking the universe in its eyes,
And what grows once never leaves,
What leaves once, never lives,
Such common sight, such cruel sight,
Oh, I could never forget the tale of your hair.

37

Yes

Under the silk she hides
the finest cloth of a weaver's mind.

38

I Have Seen The Stars Wake At Night

I have seen the stars wake at night,
when I kissed you under the moonlight,
like everything else, they fell from their prime,
and I looked at the world falling at your sight.
Through you the sun and moon rose, and,
in you was the rose that was white,
thus, when I held you in my arms,
I saw myself in a lovely plight[1].
Yesterday I saw you walk in my solitude,
and with your lips lit the lamp bright;
with your lamp I lit every firework,
and I saw them challenge sun's might.

When you would sleep like a lovely life,
and be dreaming of the greatest height,
I'd see you open your eyes suddenly.
I have seen the stars wake at night.

[1.] a dangerous situation

39

She Is Much More

She thinks god didn't make her perfect,
yet under her shadow I find everything intact;
and she uses scents, lipstick and eyeliners.
Oh, how do I tell her that she carries,
the natural scent in her body, roses on her lips,
and universe in her eyes.
She is not the one I loved.
She is much more, she is much more.

When in my dreams she laughs and walks away from me,
I chase her but our distance remains the same.
And then I wake up to see her walking again,
towards me, beyond me, above me, below me,
and I laugh at my stupidness for I know,
she lives in the air.
She is not the one I loved.
She is much more, she is much more.

She has closed her heart and I have to open it with truth,
for without her what am I if not a dictionary of pain.
Where is that key to that heart if not in the efforts made?
I will cling to her like the old man to his home.
With that being said, I wish to see the smile,
that when smiles smiles with music of the earth.

With her I will walk to the lost mountains and seas,
then I will laugh again for everything lost,
that was never claimed rests in her.
She is not the one I loved.
She is much more, she is much more.

40

My Heart Opens Like A Flower In Rain

My heart opens like a flower in rain when I think of you:
and all the time, my heart is open, waiting for you.
But, I never see you coming or even a ray of hope shining,
in the darkness I call life.
Once, in my youngness I promised to write happy poems only,
now to write for happiness is writing for you: I do not have either.

Since, I am but a poet you think not of,
I try to find reasons to cry at night;
I am waiting for you to give me a reason,
to weep and drink and cry and sing,
but of me you think not:
not even enough to sense existence and distance.

Oh, this was not the time for a poet to be born,
the world where muses read seldom the poem:
I wish to die than living this faithless lie.
And still at nights, I wonder why,
you love the poems, and not see the poet cry.

You have read me from distance,
and I have seen you from closest;
but, we were from different trees,
thus, we never truly met.

On leaves I wrote so deeply of you,
yet, you washed your feet in the green grass,
while autumn came and my tree of poems died.
Oh, who is to blame? Who is to blame?

You saw not maybe it was you every word written for,
every letter was sent for, and every cry cried for.
Or maybe you knew and cared not for me or the book,
I had written by the pen drenched in my blood,
that lovingly died to become a part of your existence:
how sad you never accepted it.

Of all the rhymes I have written,
it is this simplicity and freeness that can get me close to you:
for they both were made from you;
like I was made from sadness and hope.
In your non-existent love I found heaven and I lived:
oh, oh, oh, oh, fools are never welcome here.

Oh, look another joke has been written again,
how shall this one end?
With your smile turning cities into a garden?
Or your laugh laughing me into destruction?
How will it end? How will it end?
My heart opens like a flower in rain.

41

Solitary Flower

In this vast happy garden,
you stand, O solitary flower.
All passers become poets:
oh, one need not know anything,
to see your beauty.
Simple flower in the simple field,
with sun looking down upon you,
and earth looking up to you:
you are their solitary child, O solitary flower.

And I of the many travellers,
housed outside your field:
and you see me not, you see no one.
Just a flower, no fruit, no wind,
no roots, no shade, just a flower:
upon whose stillness my world trembles,
and I write.

When everyone leaves and no one,
is left to water you, O solitary flower,
I shall cut every vein,
and see you grow of me,
so last, but last,
we become one.

42

To Muse

Thus began the end,
with her smile lost in the flowers,
and the flowers lost in her smile.
I, like a lover,
sat and read the poems,
that I wrote for her eyes;
wishing to resurrect her from the dark abyss,
but, no I did not see her silhouette
waving through the white night.
And I being a poet to my muse,
sat there burning every paper left,
and washing every word with water,
to erase the memories of each kiss,
and each whisper and breath.

And no, I could not forget the lost love,
neither a moment nor a sight of her posing
and waiting for me to pen down her innocence.
I knew for the better part that I could not
remember the thought of forgetting her,
for how do you imagine a life without wine,
and water at the same time?
Thus, I decided: I shall leave the world
that was rejected by my love,

and take a leap and walk into the heaven,
to find her back and live with her.

At dawn I woke up to begin the dusk of my life:
I said farewell to flowers and trees
that were watered through her scarlet lips.
And there I saw a rose:
to which the idea of beauty bowed,
bowing to the fading moon;
the grief that I suffered, affected everything,
for her empyrean[1] light gave hope to all.
"This flower that was once loved by my muse,"
I thought as I pulled it from its roots:
"shall never be withered by time."
And by that, I held it in hand, and
swallowed it to my gut, hoping that
it shall feed on my body after I die,
and the flower that once was a child of muse,
shall never till I find her back: die.

Then as the sun rose like a distant kite,
I adorned the painting of my muse with vermillion[2],
and a rosary of dead flowers that shall bloom in her presence.
I looked into her eyes and without any thought,
just looked, and stared without the sound of a leaf mating with
ground;
in silence, I looked deep, and found her looking for me:
and the poet in me had been wounded,
for my muse was disoriented and wandering like a child,
looking for her house in the city of intellects.

[1.] heavenly, [2.] red pigment

I could not stop anymore, the time had come;
I walked to the sea, where she used to bathe,
and I looked at the vast sapphire, and the waves broke at the
seashore;
the sea mourns by laughing, and the trees by howling,
while I mourn by sacrificing myself to a trance that shall lead
anywhere.
Thus, I walked into the sea, without any suffering,
I lost my breath in a moment; the sea was empty,
but, now no more: there I rest on the land of sea,
with my eyes staring at the soundless heaven to where I am
headed.

43

I Recall You

Oh, I recall you,
Like a finger remaining still in memory of the ring.
Then, I found you in all things that were vast,
it is now these houses and oldness that give birth to your thought.
I cry in my house remembering you,
and it echoes a lovely music:
only the empty echoes, only the empty echoes.

Like the only cloud in my sky you stood,
and the winds blew you like a lost feather,
now I search for you, marking the sky,
making it dark and sad.
Once your direction was called home,
what is your direction now?

I wish you had left me like an inn instead,
so at least someone could have stayed in me,
so at least something would have moved in me,
but, we were a home, and no one lives
in a home that recalls memory of itself,
all the tables here, the typewriter, the cigarettes,
recall you, like I do each moment without knowing,
and each time I do, I touch my finger,
slowly and silently.

44

Health, Harmony and Happiness!

The pain I feel while writing these poems,
is immense, glorious and royal,
but, I still adorn it with my storytelling,
such that it tells of a life,
such that when you read it you smile;
these are not anecdotes of hatred,
these are not an attempt to win something,
these are just as they are,
they want to help you but they can't,
perhaps, a momentary smile,
in a lifetime of darkness and sadness,
but, that's not enough is it?
And what's enough after all, dear poem?
When even you feel you are not.

What was meant to be the brightest star,
for our earthly manners became,
a broken, torn, dying wrist of blood, blood,
let us blame the patriarchy,
let us blame the torn flesh of myriad women,
let us blame her beauty,
let us blame the women for being.
And thus, my brightest star for whom I stepped,
and walked this earth that I loathe,

became nothing and nothing, but a buried stone,
that I still seek among flowers.

This is where I take my hands off poetry,
and step under the shadow of reality,
so each woman born tomorrow shall never,
fall in the same lifeless hole again,
may no woman go without eating again,
may no woman starve herself,
may no woman cut her wrists with blade,
may no woman lose herself,
on the road of approval of the half-men,
may no woman make decisions,
that dishonour her or her grace in any way,
may no woman look in the mirror,
and throw a stone at her own fiery reflection,
may no woman be born, dear poem,
be born and be torn, day by day, like you.

And I had no dreams, I really did not,
it's just that certain white nights,
paint pictures in my eyes and I am not to blame,
I really do not have control,
over what god wants me to see and do,
so, if you ever believe me,
do believe that I wanted nothing more than love,
nothing more than existence,
nothing more than your laugh and ecstasy,
but, who ever believes nowadays.
And at times I have seen the lovely reddish mornings,
when a certain sunlight was falling,
behind my back and lighting up the room in life,

and you simply sleeping silently,
right in front of my eyes as I heard a certain music,
and you right there, the disquiet one,
sleeping, in health, harmony and happiness,
you woke up, or maybe you did not,
but, you slept in health, harmony and happiness!

But, then I wake up to find that I slept on my hand,
under the same pillow that smells,
of a scent that only my visions could've brought,
that only god wants me to smell.
So, perhaps you too are happy, perhaps you will remain,
and I hope you will always be so,
because I'm selfish, and I really don't want to be sad,
and for some reason I always,
feel a sudden funeral play in between my eyes,
and the world stops when you are sad.
Oh, I have stopped the world enough, enough
lived life like a silent mourner,
weeping and screaming in self at a flute,
that was never played.

45

I Fall In The Silence

I was silently sleeping by the river,
while taciturn[1] flowers did shiver,
the river sang like the mild rain,
the moon rose to kiss in the night's pain,
wind that hauled[2] was now ceasing,
when the trees were but appeasing,
the breeze that walked from miles,
carrying flowers and myriad smiles.
And one by one each of them fell in silence,
as my solitude was peopled, pierced was the defiance[3].

There in distance I saw a consolation to nature walk,
by the river where one did seldom talk,
her each step abated[4] our distance,
thus, my heart flew, I became aware of existence.
The winds that resisted touching my skin,
were now kissing their lost kin,
flowers were opening in the night,
and through their petals rose the light,
that kissed the moon's scars,
and he shone brighter than the stars.
Flowers rose through the soul of the rock,
in the sky flew the forgotten flock.

[1] shy, [2] pulled with force, [3] resistance, [4] reduced

And it all went by so fast,
I saw myself change at last.

Weaved by the strings of poems rested pale,
her skin that disinterred[1] my dale[2],
from her face it crept past the neck,
and her soul lived in each solitary fleck[3],
as it went down the crevice where was the breath,
that was promised to be gained after death.
Down I went as the time stood still,
and my memory was lost in her staring shrill[4].

Near me rested a tiny trough silently,
as she came and stepped in it violently,
the moon's reflection that rested still in the night,
flickered in a restless plight,
created by her and her unjudged steps;
as to a mother an infant clasps,
the trough[5] to her shadow, surrounded by blue,
then all the unseen birds flew,
to the trough, nay: a sea,
that sufficed every plea,
and the river but a mere hand,
in the giant universe of water and land.

If I had seen her eyes that night,
or touched her skin in the light,
would have I touched eternity or more,
or reached my sadness' shore.
But, to remember her like a memory,
I can create what I couldn't see.

---

[1] dig up, [2] a valley, [3] a very small patch of colour or light, [4] piercing voice, [5] an open container
for water

Each night I sit by the river,
while the taciturn flowers shiver,
to see her bathe with her scars,
and the river, a stairway of broken stars.
I still think of her in nature's compliance,
and like everything else I fall in the silence.

46

You Are Here

You are here and I am never leaving you,
you are far, but you are here,
hear me so you smile again,
for every word of mine is yours,
what I do, what I am,
is you and everything about you,
reflects in my words and they become you.

Perhaps, it is of our distance
why I feel of you so immensely,
or it is just that I have been found
in your thoughts, not in your thoughts.
Let my soul fly to the garden of your smile,
and I shall build a house in it,
with my name, so it will hold every root,
of every flower, till breath of life lasts,
so your smile remains, even when we don't.

At times I laugh why you tell me not of your past,
or your dreams, or your problems, or yourself,
I wait like a lake, for you to throw all your cursed coins in me,
so I rise up, high in bliss, hoping for you to swim in me.
Of all your sadness I shall make a ribbon,
and adorn my box of letters with it,

so when you open the box, happiness will rain,
with your sadness leaving for farther lands,
where grief isn't beautiful,
and where you do not reside.

Where shall all this take me?
Each night I walk to your city,
and in the burning May summer I am left stranded,
by a stranded highway, oh come like the brightest light,
so at least I wake up in the room I rot in.

When you ignore me, you ignore a hope,
nay: the hope, the lost hope,
hope of a universe of happiness and togetherness,
of earth blooming with faith and sky raining with love,
of your immortality and endless smiles,
of your beauty and simple nights,
and! of my unseen, sad, comical smile.
When you ignore me, you ignore yourself.

Even though you are so far and you know me,
I am yet to be known, like you,
know me perhaps by showing yourself,
the way to the city standing hollow in market of world,
so, when we meet eye to eye, to you I say:
you are here, and I am never leaving you.

47

Let Me Preserve You Like A Song

Let me preserve you like a song.
So I listen to you when I like,
and in the forest of my soul,
your tune shall echo in the pine;
words of your song, that I hear,
shine as the sun upon wintry frost;
every string that cries, cries
for what I wonder, my desire:
a song upon whose silence the world howls,
upon whose verses the rivers stop,
upon whose dance the flowers blush,
upon whose meaning I tremble.
Yet, every string cries, with every string
shivering, my whole instrument shivers,
for you are what I am:
when your tune is happy,
I echo through the streets,
when your tune is sad,
I echo in myself;
my emptiness, is from your emptiness,
I am from you, we are one song,
playing in different gatherings,
seeking the same destination,
to play at the same time,

till our surroundings become one,
and we come to life,
standing, stranded, secluded songs,
singing in self, with song becoming silence,
and eyes becoming speakers,
blushes becoming answers,
love becoming language,
sadness becoming past.
Let me preserve you like a song.

48

I Crave

I crave to be the face that looks at your face each day,
till each day ends not without me smiling at your face,
and your eyes closing upon my eyes where you rest,
so your lips know I am a gardner, admiring a garden;
with such intimacy, shall I embrace you, oh love,
that everything that left you shall emerge in you,
till you be filled with but a childhood happiness,
and all your broken words shall be spoken from me,
with all the promises that broke you once,
your future and happiness shall rest on my chest,
where your innocent head smiles, adorned by a garland.
Is it a crime, oh is this a crime, distant desire?
To be not yours, yet be yours.
Both of our emptiness, can only end together,
the time for words is over, you are my language now.

49

She Smiled (A Description)

On the garden path, in the golden evening,
I was walking on the leaves gleaming,
with death in autumn and silently weeping,
for somewhere far, a life was reaping,
a field, in spring, dying for a few roses,
while I remained admiring the poses,
of the young feather's eternal pirouette[1],
and beyond my sight a calm silhouette,
was moving with freedom and bliss in self,
whilst, I stood reading from my shelf,
that lived in dust of time and knowledge,
hoping for the world to acknowledge,
of all it wants to say, and couldn't say,
but, the people stood admiring the ray,
of light that for eyes created such lining,
that even I, the crier, saw the shining,
soul through the blackness of the painting,
then I wept, time had come of lamenting.

The bright sun shone, such that evening was red,
and all the woes of mine, seemed to me dead,
for I had found a meaning, that was not found,
in this life of wandering the world around,

---

[1] an act of spinning on one foot

but, oh it was now the poem was really recited,
when the flawless silhouette was sighted,
whose dreams now seem mine, and mine her eyes,
that shall hear all of my unheard cries;
oh, the gardens and flowers, flowers and gardens,
and know when this bitter thorn hardens,
it seeks the light of these young smiling flowers,
that innocently seem calmer than bowers:
to have described you, as flowers and nature,
I wish to measure your eye's curvature,
so I know you, your soul, your heart, your skin,
and know the idea of beauty, your kin[1];
of the radiance that flows through your breath,
shall resurrect me on the verge of death,
for it was promised to be residing in paradise,
and I gained it before the last vice;
perhaps, I should walk closer to your side,
and under your garment, take pride,
that shall be solitary the coin for the boatman,
for I will have touched god's yen[2].

It is, oh, autumn, it is, cruel, sad, it is,
the sadness' and nature's one true kiss,
that we see with falling leaves on the ground,
and hear their hysterical[3] dying sound:
but, what shall I say of my shaking legs,
while in distance to you my heart begs,
all the beauty that poets write in day and night,
is this nature, wind, grass and light,
but, what of your eyes that shine so bright,
I remember not, the painful dark plight[4]:

[1]. one's family, [2]. yearning, [3]. uncontrolled, [4]. dangerous situation

thus, I say, it is you and you, I was born for,
to remind ages of beauty's little shore,
that only I saw and cherished among the sun,
the stars, the gardens, the sky, and shun,
the beauty that was found in the trees,
for I breathed the breath of spring breeze.
And, so I walked, on the stone, to the rose,
to offer it my rusty vault of woes,
that I gave birth to, I wonder, whence[1],
but, answer was here, I walked, hence:
and then it was the sun who shone brightly,
while the dying evening cried lightly,
as the birds began singing of the spring,
and children went flying through the swing,
as the old men, began walking again,
and the ponds were delighted with rain,
the lost lovers met each other on the grass,
as the old stains fell from the glass:
I saw my flesh calmly gather on my sad face,
and fill my universe with a starry space,
I smiled, oh yes, in heart I was smiling,
for in the dead sunset sea, a wave was rising.

I was walking in the direction to meet her,
and test my love whose loves never were,
or touch the skin that softly screamed,
what all painters never dreamed,
or just take a glance in her universe,
through the eyes that begin a verse
so free and simple that it is forgotten,
each time recited, with smiles of rotten,

[1] from where

ones that no one ever touched or kissed,
in her light, even they are missed.
Or, if possible, just see her loving smile,
and smile back, thinking all the while,
of future with her, in her, nothing beyond her,
then I reached the tree she was standing under,
and I said, with the sea and falling scarlet sun:
"We are alone, we are together, we are one."
And oh, she heard my words loud and clear,
and sensed at once, my innocent fear,
that breathed on my past and lived on tomorrow,
so, she turned around, and smiled my sorrow,
for what else was to be achieved in this world,
other than this girl, by flowers, who was pearled,
and what answer could she have given me,
I knew it all, I knew it all, yet couldn't see,
all the books at this moment were lying,
for your poet's happiness was prying,
his own self, it had never before seen,
then, I saw the answer: I was left serene:
she smiled, and said not, oh she just smiled,
nothing was said, she said nothing, she smiled.

.

50

Justification

Oh, no it was not about the hair on the legs,
Or the gaps between the thighs that were your dream,
No, it was of course not about the make-up that
Added a little more sunshine to a star's gleam,
It was not for the flat stomach or the hourglass waist,
And even the mono-brow or no-brow which of beauty scream.
Yes, oh yes! Very yes! Most delightful and strongest yes!
These lights of beauty flow like flowers in its stream,
And to you it seems dead and unwanted whilst,
I see it as the river of existence, art and oblivion.

So, when you think your face is deformed or you have horse-teeth,
Know that all these curses were product of magic
That bit by bit, piece by piece, day by day,
Formed something that I could look at till I could,
Know that hair on your legs is like grass in a garden,
Your broken nails are wars that you've lost against yourself,
The scarlet lipstick is a row of roses in this courtyard,
With fallen lilies everywhere that grow further everyday,
You should stop blaming them for a few dry thorns,
That hurt the ones—like me—who visit you.

Want what you want and flaunt what you have,
For the world don't move even a strand of your hair,
For yourself, move mountains, storms and seas,

Because yes, the sea waves come far from the shore
To kiss your feet in sand and sense her heart.

And look gently in the mirror and you'll see it is looking at you,
Like I am looking at you whilst you read and smile.
It was not for your face, or eyes, or what I had not seen,
It was all for you, simply, tragically, completely serene.

51

Union

The city with pink wind blowing through sunsets,
Woke up with summer rain singing in the sky,
The petrichor[1] that was lost in the smell of factories,
Was found hiding in the dew of young flowers,
That opened before the sunrise to kiss the seas,
And the grass that was never touched by the dew,
Bathed in the same rain as all of Beauty,
And one by one each life became but one.

Certain love-birds took flight in the showering sky,
While the troughs became lakes adorned by a waterfall,
"When Nature is waking up all lives, why are you asleep?"
Wondered your young poet glancing on the street,
And the answer was there in uncertainty: Rain was free.
Oh, the free Rain could bring a storm or love on land,
What can I say to the cowards hiding in their rooms?
What can I wish to see if not union of beloved and Rain?

And yes, there was a distance that separated us,
But, this rain touched her as much as it touched me,
And she too perhaps looked in the distance seeking bliss,
The bliss that she desires be indulged with freedom,

[1] smell of the first rain

Just like I was looking in the misty rain for her silhouette,
By that she was there as raindrops kissed my eyes,
She stood there right by my side smiling,
The cities watched us defying distance with thoughts.

She had been in me perhaps forever hiding from herself,
And this rain blessed her to show her freedom rests in me;
What was this that I had at last gained at dawn?
A happy life or a future forlorn?
We had united through language,
Like my words touch your eyes, rain touches your lips,
And I, your poet, in my words rest in your eyes.

This rain is but cruel for it soon shall end,
But, oh, here we are at last just staying still,
I shall not expect anything of you at this moment,
Let this be but the first moment beyond language,
To describe: this rain, you and you in this rain,
This rain shall again unite us at dawn,
For then only we are awake, only we are alone,
And then only we shall be alive.

52

Rain

Who is that bathing on the street, under the rain,
And, oh, even the sun has joined the rain,
To glance at this free statue of Beauty,
Her hair, so close to itself hides flowers and stars,
Her eyelids, when they are lifted reveal life,
In eyes that no one could ever ignore,
For this is all one wishes to see before the fall.

And there are her lips that house water in them,
With her waist the raindrops have kissed all,
Oh, her naked pale feet stepping in troughs,
That are full of countless stars born by
The union of sun and rain:
Eternity! Disinterred by her feet.

From the seas that travelled in white clouds,
Gliding over fields, becoming bowers[1],
Uniting in a city with other clouds,
Falling upon people, playfully joining rivers,
And some drops of these touching her,
Oh! to have travelled through seas, sun and time,
And falling at your feet in a trough,
Living with stars: is that not my dream?

[1.] shady place under trees

53

No Words

And no words shall hold this moment,
It is your eyes, my eyes and silence,
Nothing to lose there is nothing to gain,
We are a part, we can never be apart,
For here is a promise written with words,
Becoming free by being short of words,
From my field of words you have stolen flowers,
And thus, making me common like else:
How beautiful, lovely I feel now that I,
Know not which star wants to be your eye.

Let this not be remembered, let this not be described,
Let this moment just live in your eyes and my eyes,
Beyond and past here the sorrows live and sing,
Beyond and past here words take back the power,
Just this moment of our eyes meeting innocently,
Rests still while lives continue to live or slowly die.
Now we will always be together in this world or another,
Always in dreams, reality, time, memories, voices,
With quill quilted with forlorn petals, I shall write,
The last poem which till the end we shall recite.

54

Silence

You belong to the sun, the moon, the stars, the water.
A ship of beauty and innocence that fled,
Spilled a few drops in the ocean,
And carried in clouds, you flew,
To my doorstep and you fell.
Hereby, I shall correct the mistake,
And take you back to the oceans,
Where sea and sun unite,
Oh that little green shore,
Where flowers seldom grow,
You will find all life in your shadow,
While you bathe in the sunlight.
I will then see the picture of all words,
Thus, what use is this pen if it can't describe you.

I will gently, calmly smile,
For words are lost in their meanings,
And you are beyond all meanings,
You are made of silence.

55

If You Have The Courage Of Walking

If you have the courage of walking,
A life awaits you,
Resting in a dark room,
That if you walk in, be adorned by lights,
Following your feet the floor be a bed of roses,
Where we can lie down watching lights flicker on the ceiling,
If you have the courage of walking,
If you can still walk out your room,
I will leave my door open,
In summer, rain, winter and storms,
I will seek always beyond the gates,
In the chirping of the birds,
The fragrance of the flowers,
The colours of the butterflies,
Sound of your footsteps breaking leaves.
If you have the courage of walking,
Or even to walk beyond your room,
In your night clothes when people sleep,
To look into the hollow night:
In depths that night never knew,
I may not stop weaving the tales,
Writing poems or painting pictures,
So, if one day you walk in the night,
I will give you a world full of yourself.

If you have the courage of walking,
One step, one smile, one tear,
Can help you escape your room,
Where you are alone, yet lost;
One step, one smile, one tear,
Can set it on a fire from within:
You are my fire from within.

When I had just closed my doors,
A smoke made its way through my windows,
One step, one smile, one tear,
And you will be here;
One step, one smile, one tear,
And we will be here.

56

Come Back To Me, Dear Poem

Come back to me, dear poem
when you're sure of yourself,
when it is the last time you come
to anyone, to any other place.
When every doubt in your life ceases,
and you come out of your rose
to realise it never existed,
when all the demons of the past
flicker in the past
and not burn in today.

Come back to me, dear poem
I don't know you, really,
but I knew someone like you,
someone who had something
that was taken from someone:
someone:
someone who was taken
from time;
if you still have the fire that
the patriarchy, the sadness,
the dark rooms, the blades,
burnt;
the fire that in my eyes still burns,

if there are some embers left,
then come back to me, dear poem,
so least, but least we can light
the cigarette of our souls with them.

Come back to me, dear poem
when you become what you wanted
when you finally stand on your feet
when all we have to do is: live.
I cannot help you in this war of yourself,
because if I do, then you would still lose,
and thus, I would lose too.
So, fight for yourself, and you'll see,
when you win, oh you will see,
how the crown of lights will settle
around your head, how liquid stars
will slide down your hair.

Come back to me, dear poem
so we can give back to the generations
what the generations took from time.

57

Are We Heading Home

Are we heading home or were we heading home?
Are we even moving or are we standing still
in the sunset of our youngness?
It is a higher sadness that leads to a certain maturity,
a certain calmness that rests in balconies, verandahs[1],
where we see the afternoon in siesta[2],
but what if we found in the youngness,
what if an entire universe worked to make two lives,
that were not to meet, meet,
and know each other like they knew each other,
what if we had that, what if we saw that,
what if we knew that and what if we ignored that,
and what if that is the reason,
to every problem, every issue, every sadness,
whatever walked in our lives,
because our lives are sad,
blue lives, blue lights, red lives, red lights,
flowerless lives, talking about flowers,
you are the flower, and where am I?
I miss you, and you are there everywhere,
I leave towns, I leave cities,
I change names, I meet girls,
pretty, pretty, beautiful, but each time

[1.] a roofed platform along the outside of a house, [2.] rest or nap

in my life, at every step something remains the same,
one thing remains: you.
So what if we ignored what the universe conspired,
but at least we could meet, at least we could not hurt each
other.
Oh, the times are so fragile,
the clock is ticking,
for everything to depart.

58

Lifeless Life

As much as the sun couldn't overpower,
So much that distance couldn't perish,
Vast as the point where sight disappears,
So much that expression became hollow,
And so strong that it could be felt,
That is how much I loved you.
And now I can only forgive and forget,
The lifeless life that I never knew.

59

You're Not A Muse

You're not a muse[1], you're not a line,
Or a song that in words I confined.

You are in existence, alive and strained,
By those eyes of people on the road,
While you desire but a gentle, calm rain,
That hands leading to cars never showed.

And I know you vomit, I know you cry,
You smile seldom, and mostly hide,
Your scars that with each question die,
So on you dream of the last tide.

Forgotten are the half-thought novels that I never wrote,
If they bring to you any such disgrace,
That I not write the place in wind that each eyelash remote,
Lives before it slides down the face.

And forgotten are the loves that never knew love,
In its nakedness under shadow of sadness,
But, rather dreamt further of you, stars and skies above,
That they saw, not felt and couldn't express.
And if we be in vicinity[2]—oh, the two lifeless lives that live,
In sadness under every happy weather—

[1.] a person who inspires art, [2.] the area near a particular place,

Perhaps, to happiness a gentle lesson we would give,
By being if not happy, then least sad together.

You're not a muse, you're not a line,
We were put in being to strive[1].
Are you the girl I fell for?
Are you there? Are you still alive?

[1] struggle

60

There Was Once A Girl

There was once a girl, silent and subtle,
Who through her words made fire still.
And some claimed to have died for her,
But, none did she ever kill.

She strolled like a butterfly through melancholy,
Making the tasteless air into fragrance.
But, she disappeared yet garden remained colourful,
And every room of air shivered at each glance.

And she had dreams so huge and vast,
That to her listeners they would spread,
Like candle-light in a dark room,
Burning their own fires in the red.

But, she was at times gentle and mostly rude,
For demons conquered her and I conclude:
All that she was, she was all for herself,
A decaying weather, a changing mood.

61

Into The Light

And now I am looking forward to the life,
that I always had, but never saw,
I am looking straight into the light and
a thousand voices are calling me.
I am scared.

The life that I always had, the life of me;
one that I couldn't live without a thought,
of a certain lie that I would create,
I am going to live the life lieless right now.

Everything is passing by so fast,
I feel you are departing from my window,
And that's all I ever had, to be honest,
a window fogged by distance and desire.

But, the train is now moving, and you are there,
it's as if somebody is flipping the page
in an album that told the story of ages,
the page that was so long, that it took so long
to merely turn itself over and let me look over.

It's moving, you're staying still, in the silence
singing the wordless melodies that were born through me,
I am looking forward to the next station, full of love and sadness,
you were never here, you will always remain standing there.

62

Death

That day I remember, that day I recall,
When I saw the marks of blade on her wrists,
Then those long nights grew longer,
And I found myself crawling in the depths,
Of a mind that did not know itself,
Or lost its conscience by whips of eyes,
Either way I too was free-falling,
Between cities that were so far apart,
That her hope became my home.

And what could I even do after that,
She who died long ago was alive,
And I who lived for a certain definition,
Of a word that she altered one day,
Was feeding on the universal connection,
That her reality couldn't understand.

Then, she who hurt herself limitlessly,
Cut out a smile from existence,
By finding a path more available and easy,
And I, who saw the life of lights,
Was left burning under its massive shadow,
For it was not to live for me,

It was not for anybody, it was a death,
For itself, and for others to see.

But, I yet was hanging between music,
And unheard melodies that cried,
Of a certain world I created in myself,
That mourned each time she died.
She changed death into her undying friend,
And woke him up each time she fell,
While I stood in the distance giving hand,
To another hand that never held.

She continued to come back, and leave
When she felt the rush of reality,
But, she continued to die night by night,
Or maybe she did not, I don't know,
How can I know anything outside of me?
She did change my life and meanings,
Then death was like a crop of wheat standing,
In a barren field, under the windless sky.

63

You Are Not Mine

You are not mine, I know
you are not yours either;
but, I hope you hear from
my words the love and fear
that fill my soul with
the thought of you.

Party ends after the night,
and then there is light
of the day that hurts the eye,
the eye that was nurtured,
in the dark room that now echoes
the murmurs of the girl
that left her home seeking the
light beyond the curtains.

But, the room will always remain
for time created it in you,
and time can only open its walls
that reflect blood sliding
down from the foot of a picture
like it slid down the wrist,
like the tears slide down the eye
spreading eyeliner in pain.

Take your time, and brick by brick
break it with your fists that
you will nurture in light of those
thousand sunsets when you would
come home alone, after working and
being the woman you dreamt of
being, and the woman you always were
in my gentle, sad, unseen eye.

See, I am very simple, I have become
what I desired very long ago:
the man who could stain the leaf of
time with the fragile ink
that flowed like a river under the skin;
I became that long before you,
it is just that I want to be even more,
now that I have known you.

You and I share some secrets that I
have kept hidden under words,
and characters that are 'her' and
'you:' all of them are you,
all of them come from you, my every
smile comes from you and you
think you are nothing but a mere story,
oh my god! what a tragedy.

I cannot help what you think, and you
cannot know what I ever wanted,
but I know why I did everything I did
and do you know what was it?
The secret that makes my rivers stop,

that makes the birds chirp low,
that makes the sun hide behind curtain,
that joins the cities like stars:

What I could never say, because time
was never right for you to hear,
but time is a road that we walk on
that suddenly disappears and we
find ourselves either old or dead;
so here on, under our distance,
and on the road where we never were,
I say to light falling on you:

I respect you, I believe in you,
I am very proud of you and
I love you, deeply, entirely I do
I love you and I can't say
for I don't know where you are now
so I say here on paper that:
I love you, last desire, I love you,
become your own, be around me.

But, now what, where are you and
who are you; do I know you?
Did I ever even know you or did we
always join the same stars
with our fingers that only made
sound on screens that scream
still of the distance we defied
with a connection disconnected.

So, now do I still wait or do I
not wait anymore? I ask this

to myself, not to you for you can
only give me a certainty and
truth that can flourish or destroy
a life that never was reality;
but, hanging in between the two,
I suffocate, I suffocate.

I love you, deeply, entirely I do,
break it with your fists that
the man who could stain the leaf of
light beyond the curtains,
come home alone, after working and
what I desired very long ago:
I love you, last desire, I love you,
I say to light falling on you:

You are not mine, I know
you are not yours either;
but, I hope you hear from
my words the love and fear
that fill my soul with
the thought of you,
the thought you thought
I loved more than you.

64

Poem

I wait for you, days, nights,
Falling, falling between sights.

65

Farewell

Farewell, O muse: I have wept,
Enough for thy[1] eyes,
That seem far and farther,
From my comical cries,
And hide in the rose of Beauty,
Filled with all the lies.

Creeping past the hours of nights,
Was I doing the lovely sin,
Of calling the midnight moon,
Upon my oblivion of gin[2],
Yet, no word of mine was heard,
And broken was the dream to win.

Holding flowers in my young hands,
I thought I had a name,
Among these gardens and grass,
But, I was put to shame,
By fate's very saddening flute,
That none could ever blame.

[1.] your, [2.] alcohol

Turning and twisting words a-changing,
Languages created by ages,
For a beauty I had sighted in distance,
Who put me in cage of its cages,
And left me to rot or bloom I thought,
I silently wept Beauty through ages.

Much of pain that I would gain,
Was destined by my hand,
So, I would shine through the pine,
And bring stars to the land,
So, you would see your lovely name,
Written with stars and sand.

But, of all the readers that read me best,
You became another one,
That read and yet not read the soul,
Of poet whom you shun[1],
If you had seen you'd see your face,
Shining brighter than the sun.

Where ones who print the papers,
Can put any to shame,
Oh, what of the papers I wrote,
Extending thy deity's[2] name,
That gave me sleepless nights,
And put me to the blame.

[1] ignore [2] goddess'

And when I walk this old city,
That sparkles with dust,
I seek the shadow where lives,
The sacred light of Lust,
As I find the sleeping Beauty,
I am sent flying by a gust.

The simplicity that was sacrificed,
I stole it from your smile,
And I stood tall in the market of words,
Casting all the while,
Your face that roses kept to chase,
By the clouds in exile.

Was I so small or was I so big,
I wrote vast for one breath,
That I could never gain or lose,
Or quilt it with my wrath,
Then for doing the eternal sin,
Fall in the abyss of death.

My words that you might love to read,
Have never before been read,
By the scarlet princess of dawn,
But, when you read my words in red,
The yellow rose through the blue,
And my sorrows were dead.

Or so I thought I had found it all,
That one could never find,
But, oh you put my words to trial,
And owned my body and mind,
To walk and rest and rest and walk,
Till I became but blind.

My eyes that fell from the hell,
Were cursed to see your sight,
And dwell[1] to tell the dreams,
That were adorned[2] by the Light,
But, dreams always end with tears,
And the life becomes a plight.

Oh, what can a dream do at most,
It can steal from you reality,
Immortal dreams written with ink,
Can take away all the clarity,
That was gifted by almighty,
And was lost in your sanctity[3].

Where could these poems lead me,
To a land where you are,
Oh, so I write with my broken heart,
And begin to walk far,
Far from myself and leave all I am,
To stand by the brightest star.

[1] live, [2] decorated, [3] quality of being sacred

I know not where I am headed,
To a giant dark mountain,
Or a waterfall singing at night,
Or perhaps, to a rain,
Of a tomorrow where I can smile,
When words go not in vain.

When I would also tell the tales,
Or at least once a story,
That I lived and that I felt,
Was a part of my glory,
That simply came not in being,
From me being observatory.

And I looked at all the angles,
That your waist entwined,
And changed the idea of Science,
And gave eyes to the blind,
But, was I the only one you hurt,
Or more lost their mind?

Maybe you were created to hurt,
The ones who offer love,
So you would be not limited,
To any sky above,
But, it ceases its freedom,
For sky loves the dove.

A last time I sing to thee[1],
Hear, love, hear me,
I wish to take you to nature,
And make you see,
That only with my hand,
Can you totally be free.

But, you will see not what I want,
And I will do what I do,
To continue to walk in blue,
Nights when howls coo,
A sweet music that leads to,
The moon that is you.

But, at times in pain I wonder,
You are here yet not near,
To close my eyes I can see you,
To open them, oh, I fear,
Oh, disorientation is my life,
In dreams you are here.

So, I wait for you may walk in life,
Hoping you will embrace,
My soul, my body and my mind,
And free me from the disgrace,
That muses give me always,
Through their faces I cannot face.

[1] you

Farewell, O muse: I have wept,
Enough for thy eyes,
That seem far and farther,
From my comical cries,
And hide in the rose of Beauty,
Filled with all the lies.

Oh, I wish to write longer and better,
But, I can't yet give the best,
And you wish to not read anymore,
With a sigh I take pen off my chest,
Oh, you are free, free from my words,
And I now rest.